Please make sure to read the enclosed Ninja Owner's Guide prior to using your unit.

Nutri Ninja® | Ninja® Blender Duo™
with Auto-iQ™ Technology

Simply Delicious, Simply Nutritious

75+ DELICIOUS RECIPES

Editors and Content: Bob Warden, Meghan Reilly, Amy Golino, Kenzie Swanhart, Elizabeth Skladany, and Daniel Davis
Recipe Development: Judy Cannon and Great Flavors Recipe Development Team
Graphic Designer: Liz Parmalee and Leslie Anne Feagley
Creative Director: Lauren Wiernasz
Photography: Quentin Bacon
Additional Photography: Gary Sloan, Albie Colatonio and Heath Robbins
Food Stylist: Mariana Velasquez
Flavors Test Kitchen: Stephen Delaney, Andrea Schwob, and Bob Warden

Published in the United States of America by
SharkNinja Operating LLC
180 Wells Avenue
Newton, MA 02459

ISBN: 978-1-4951-1675-9

10 9 8 7 6 5
Printed in China

Table of Contents

Watermelon Basil Sangria,
page 89

*Extract a drink containing vitamins and nutrients from fruits and vegetables.

Simple, Delicious & Nutritious

It's easy to add more fruits, vegetables, nuts, and seeds to your diet. The Small 18-ounce, Regular 24-ounce, and Jumbo Multi-Serve 32-ounce cups with Auto-iQ™ are your tools to release the amazing power hidden within these essential foods.** The powerful Nutri Ninja® high-speed blade system unlocks these nutritious foods, turning them into silky-smooth, grit-free juices. The Auto-iQ™ Nutri Ninja® BLEND and ULTRA BLEND programs allow you to make these delicious drinks automatically at the touch of a button. With the Nutri Ninja® cups, you can also make homemade, preservative-free salad dressings, vegetable dips, and fresh fruit desserts.

To convert a Small 18-ounce Cup recipe to a Jumbo Multi-Serve 32-ounce one, multiply ingredients by 2. To convert a Regular 24-ounce Cup recipe to a Jumbo Multi-Serve 32-ounce Cup, multiply by 1.5.

**Extract hidden nutrients and vitamins by blending whole fruits and vegetables.

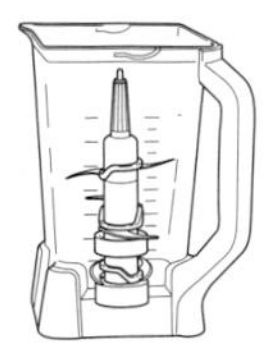

When using the large 72-ounce† Pitcher, press the Auto-iQ™ FROZEN DRINKS/SMOOTHIES button to create family smoothies and frozen cocktails. Use the Auto-iQ™ PUREE button to turn fresh vegetables, herbs, and beans into silky-smooth vegetable purees, soups, and dips.

†64 oz. max capacity

Why Nutrient Extraction*?

Nutrient extract* juices provide you with a simple way to boost your daily recommended nutritional intake. Key benefits include:

- Extracting the vitamins and nutrients in your smoothie or juice helps you get the most out of the healthy ingredients you put in it
- Helps facilitate a nutritious diet—easy way to get your daily servings of fruits and vegetables
- Great variety of ingredients, textures, and flavor options
- Can be a quick and easy meal replacement
- Easy to add more protein and "good fats"
- Leaves behind fibrous pulp unlike normal juicers

⚠ CAUTION: Remove the Nutri Ninja® Blade Assembly from the cup upon completion of blending. Some ingredients have the potential to expand after blending, resulting in excessive pressure buildup that can pose a risk of injury.

*Extract a drink containing vitamins and nutrients from fruits and vegetables.

Mix & Match Recipe Ideas

Create your own juices, smoothies, soups, dips, and sauces with these great food and flavor combos!

These Taste Great	With Any of These
Apples, pears, nut milks	Cinnamon, nutmeg, almonds, walnuts
Kale, Swiss chard, romaine	Fresh lemons, pears, kiwi, ginger
Green tea	All berries, tart cherry and pomegranate concentrates
Sweet potatoes, carrots, butternut squash	Turmeric, maple syrup
arugula	Mint, pears, apples
Pineapple, mango, papaya	Coconut, bananas
strawberries	basil, mint, goji berries

Tabbouleh Dip, page 98

Feel-Good Meal Swaps

With a few simple tweaks, you can change up your favorite recipes without losing out on flavor.

	Instead of	Substitute This
DAIRY	Evaporated milk	Evaporated skim milk
	Whole milk	1% milk, nonfat milk, almond milk
	Cheddar cheese	Low-fat cheddar cheese
	Ice cream	Frozen yogurt or sorbet
	Cream cheese	Neufchâtel or light cream cheese
	Whipped cream	Light whipped topping
	Ricotta cheese	Low-fat ricotta cheese
	Cream	Fat-free half & half, evaporated skim milk
	Sour cream, full fat	Plain low-fat yogurt, plain Greek yogurt
PROTEIN	Bacon	Canadian bacon, turkey bacon, smoked turkey, or lean prosciutto (Italian ham)
	Ground beef	Extra-lean or lean ground beef, ground chicken or turkey breast, tofu, tempeh
	Meat as the main ingredient	Three times as many vegetables as the meat on pizzas or in casseroles, soups, and stews
OTHER	Soups, creamed	Nonfat-milk-based soups, pureed carrots, potatoes, or tofu for thickening agents
	Soups; sauces; dressings; crackers; canned meat, fish, and vegetables	Low-sodium or reduced-sodium versions

	Instead of	Substitute This
GRAINS	Bread, white	Whole-grain bread
	Bread crumbs, dry	Crushed bran cereal or almond meal
	Pasta, enriched (white)	Whole wheat pasta
	Rice, white	Brown rice, wild rice, bulgur, or pearl barley
FATS	Butter, margarine, shortening, or oil in baked goods	Applesauce or prune puree for half of the butter, shortening, or oil; butter spreads or shortenings specially formulated for baking without trans fats (Note: To avoid dense, soggy, or flat baked goods, don't substitute oil for butter or shortening. Also don't substitute diet, whipped, or tub-style margarine for regular margarine.)
	Butter, margarine, shortening, or oil to prevent sticking	Cooking spray or nonstick pans
	Mayonnaise	Reduced-calorie mayonnaise-type salad dressing or reduced-calorie, reduced-fat mayonnaise
	Oil-based marinades	Wine, balsamic vinegar, fruit juice, or fat-free broth
SUGARS	Sugar	In most baked goods you can reduce the amount of sugar by one-half; intensify sweetness by adding vanilla, nutmeg, or cinnamon.
	Syrup	Pureed fruit, such as applesauce, or low-calorie, sugar-free syrup
	Chocolate chips	Dried cranberries
SAUCES	Soy sauce	Low-sodium soy sauce, tamari sauce (which is gluten-free), hot mustard
SALT	Salt	Herbs, spices, citrus juices (lemon, lime, orange), rice vinegar, salt-free seasoning mixes or herb blends, low-sodium soy sauce
	Seasoning salts (garlic, celery, or onion salts)	Herb-only seasonings, such as garlic powder, celery seed, or onion flakes, or finely chopped herbs or garlic, celery, or onions

Avocado-lada, page 10

PREP TIME: 5 minutes SERVINGS: 4–6 CONTAINER: 72-ounce Pitcher

Avocado-lada

Ingredients

2 ripe avocados, peeled, pits removed

2 small ripe bananas

4 cups coconut water

1½ cups frozen pineapple chunks

Directions

1. Place all of the ingredients into the 72-ounce Pitcher in the order listed.
2. Select Auto-iQ™ FROZEN DRINKS/SMOOTHIES.

NINJA KNOW-HOW

YOU CAN SUBSTITUTE COCONUT MILK FOR COCONUT WATER FOR AN EVEN RICHER DRINK.

PREP TIME: 5 minutes SERVINGS: 4–6 CONTAINER: 72-ounce Pitcher

Spiced Cucumber

Ingredients

2 cups chopped English cucumber

1¼ cups cantaloupe chunks

1 jalapeño, seeds removed

1 cup green seedless grapes

2 cups water

1¼ cups ice

Directions

1. Place all of the ingredients into the 72-ounce Pitcher in the order listed.
2. Select Auto-iQ™ FROZEN DRINKS/SMOOTHIES.

PREP TIME: 5 minutes **SERVINGS:** 1 **CONTAINER:** Small 18-ounce Cup

Berry Tropical Smoothie

Ingredients

¼ cup spinach

¼ cup water

¼ cup strawberries, hulled

¼ cup blueberries

½ cup mango chunks

¼ cup pineapple chunks

¼ cup ice

Directions

1. Place all of the ingredients into the Small 18-ounce Cup in the order listed.
2. Select Auto-iQ™ Nutri Ninja® ULTRA BLEND.
3. Remove blades from cup after blending.

NINJA KNOW-HOW

ADD 1 TEASPOON FRESH GINGER FOR A SPICY KICK.

PREP TIME: 5 minutes SERVINGS: 4–6 CONTAINER: 72-ounce Pitcher

The Refueler

Ingredients

2 oranges, peeled, cut in quarters, seeds removed

2 small ripe bananas

2 carrots, peeled, chopped

3¹/₄ cups almond milk

2 cups ice

Directions

1. Place all of the ingredients into the 72-ounce Pitcher in the order listed.
2. Select Auto-iQ™ FROZEN DRINKS/SMOOTHIES.

PREP TIME: 5 minutes SERVINGS: 2 CONTAINER: Jumbo Multi-Serve 32-ounce Cup

Go Cocoa

Ingredients

1¹/₂ cups unsweetened coconut milk

4 tablespoons unsweetened cocoa powder

4 tablespoons whole almonds

4 dates

2 small frozen ripe bananas, cut in half

1 cup ice

Directions

1. Place all of the ingredients into the Jumbo Multi-Serve 32-ounce Cup in the order listed.
2. Select Auto-iQ™ Nutri Ninja® ULTRA BLEND.
3. Remove blades from cup after blending.

PREP TIME: 5 minutes SERVINGS: 10–12 CONTAINER: Regular 24-ounce Cup

Call Me Popeye

Ingredients

2 dates, cut in half

1 celery stalk, cut in quarters

1 ripe kiwi, peeled, cut in half

1 cup chopped cabbage

1 cup kale

1⅓ cups hazelnut milk

1 cup ice

Directions

1. Soak the dates in 1 cup of warm water for 30 minutes. Drain, then set aside.
2. Place all of the ingredients into the Regular 24-ounce Cup in the order listed.
3. Select Auto-iQ™ Nutri Ninja® ULTRA BLEND.
4. Remove blades from cup after blending.

NINJA KNOW-HOW

SUBSTITUTE ALMOND MILK FOR HAZELNUT MILK IF PREFERRED.

PREP TIME: 5 minutes SERVINGS: 1 CONTAINER: Regular 24-ounce Cup

Broc & Roll

Ingredients

2 tablespoons broccoli sprouts

1/2 lime, peeled, seeds removed

1/4 cup celery with leaves

1/4 ripe avocado, peeled, pit removed

1/4 cup fresh parsley leaves

1 cup water

1/2 cup frozen raspberries

Directions

1. Place all of the ingredients into the Regular 24-ounce Cup in the order listed.
2. Select Auto-iQ™ Nutri Ninja® ULTRA BLEND.
3. Remove blades from cup after blending.

PREP TIME: 5 minutes SERVINGS: 4 CONTAINER: 72-ounce Pitcher

Cherry Oat Dream

Ingredients

1 apple, uncored, chopped

2 cups white cranberry juice

1 cup cooked oatmeal

2 cups frozen cherries

Directions

1. Place all of the ingredients into the 72-ounce Pitcher in the order listed.
2. Select Auto-iQ™ FROZEN DRINKS/SMOOTHIES.

PREP TIME: 5 minutes SERVINGS: 2 CONTAINER: Regular 24-ounce Cup

Lean Green Ninja

Ingredients

1/4 cup spinach

1/4 cup kale leaves

1/3 small ripe banana

1/3 cup pineapple chunks

1/3 cup mango chunks

1/3 cup water

1/4 cup ice

Directions

1. Place all of the ingredients into the Regular 24-ounce Cup in the order listed.
2. Select Auto-iQ™ Nutri Ninja® BLEND.
3. Remove blades from cup after blending.

NINJA KNOW-HOW

ADD 1 OR 2 TABLESPOONS FLAXSEED FOR AN ADDITIONAL BOOST.

PREP TIME: 5 minutes SERVINGS: 2 CONTAINER: Regular 24-ounce Cup

Gingered Acai

Ingredients

½ cup unsweetened acai berry puree, thawed

1 (.035 ounce) packet stevia

2 teaspoons fresh ginger

1½ cups pomegranate juice

2 cups frozen strawberries

Directions

1. Place all of the ingredients into the Regular 24-ounce Cup in the order listed.
2. Select Auto-iQ™ Nutri Ninja® BLEND.
3. Remove blades from cup after blending.

NINJA KNOW-HOW

YOU CAN SUBSTITUTE MIXED BERRIES OR RASPBERRIES FOR TASTY VARIATIONS.

PREP TIME: 5 minutes SERVINGS: 2 CONTAINER: Regular 24-ounce Cup

Red Devil

Ingredients

1 cup shredded red cabbage

1/4 cup chopped cucumber

1 tablespoon fresh basil leaves

2 tablespoons pomegranate juice

1 1/4 cups unsweetened apple juice

1/2 cup silken tofu

1 cup ice

Directions

1. Place all of the ingredients into the Regular 24-ounce Cup in the order listed.
2. Select Auto-iQ™ Nutri Ninja® BLEND.
3. Remove blades from cup after blending.

NINJA KNOW-HOW

ADD 2 TABLESPOONS TART CHERRY CONCENTRATE FOR A SUPER-FOOD BOOST.

PREP TIME: 5 minutes SERVINGS: 2 CONTAINER: Regular 24-ounce Cup

Pineapple Pleaser

Ingredients

2/3 cup ripe papaya, peeled, cut in chunks

1 1/4 cups original rice milk

1 tablespoon cashew butter

1 cup frozen pineapple chunks

Directions

1. Place all of the ingredients into the Regular 24-ounce Cup in the order listed.
2. Select Auto-iQ™ Nutri Ninja® ULTRA BLEND.
3. Remove blades from cup after blending.

PREP TIME: 5 minutes SERVINGS: 2 CONTAINER: Regular 24-ounce Cup

Power Ball

Ingredients

1 small ripe banana

3/4 cup unsweetened, light coconut milk

1/2 teaspoon unsweetened cocoa powder

3/4 cup frozen blueberries

Directions

1. Place all of the ingredients into the Regular 24-ounce Cup in the order listed.
2. Select Auto-iQ™ Nutri Ninja® ULTRA BLEND.
3. Remove blades from cup after blending.

PREP TIME: 5 minutes **SERVINGS:** 2 **CONTAINER:** Regular 24-ounce Cup

Purple Potion

Ingredients

3/4 cup roasted beets, chilled, cut in chunks

1 1/4 cups carrot juice

1 cup frozen blueberries

Directions

1. Place all of the ingredients into the Regular 24-ounce Cup in the order listed.
2. Select Auto-iQ™ Nutri Ninja® ULTRA BLEND.
3. Remove blades from cup after blending.

DO NOT BLEND HOT INGREDIENTS.

NINJA® KNOW-HOW

ADD 2 TEASPOONS ACAI POWDER FOR A SUPER-FOOD BOOST.

PREP TIME: 5 minutes **SERVINGS:** 2 **CONTAINER:** Regular 24-ounce Cup

Coconut Crush

Ingredients

1 small celery stalk, cut in chunks

1 ripe banana

1¼ cups unsweetened coconut milk

1 tablespoon coconut palm sugar

1 tablespoon tart cherry concentrate

1½ cups ice

Directions

1. Place all of the ingredients into the Regular 24-ounce Cup in the order listed.
2. Select Auto-iQ™ Nutri Ninja® BLEND.
3. Remove blades from cup after blending.

NINJA KNOW-HOW

ADD 1 TABLESPOON SPANISH BEE POLLEN FOR A SUPER-FOOD BOOST.

PREP TIME: 5 minutes SERVINGS: 2 CONTAINER: Regular 24-ounce Cup

Quinoa-ing You Up

Ingredients

1½ cups rice milk

½ cup cooked quinoa, chilled

¾ cup pumpkin puree

¾ teaspoon pumpkin pie spice

1 tablespoon pure maple syrup

1 cup ice

Directions

1. Place all of the ingredients into the Regular 24-ounce Cup in the order listed.
2. Select Auto-iQ™ Nutri Ninja® BLEND.
3. Remove blades from cup after blending.

DO NOT BLEND HOT INGREDIENTS.

PREP TIME: 15 minutes SERVINGS: 4 CONTAINER: 72-ounce Pitcher

Autumn Balancer

Ingredients

10 ounces steamed sweet potato, chilled

2 cups unsweetened almond milk

¼ cup maple syrup

2 teaspoons flaxseed

½ teaspoon ground turmeric

1 teaspoon salt

1½ cups ice

Directions

1. Place all of the ingredients into the 72-ounce Pitcher in the order listed.
2. Select Auto-iQ™ FROZEN DRINKS/SMOOTHIES.

DO NOT BLEND HOT INGREDIENTS.

PREP TIME: 5 minutes **SERVINGS:** 2 **CONTAINER:** Regular 24-ounce Cup

Watermelon Cooler

Ingredients

1/4 pear, cut in chunks, seeds removed

2 large fresh basil leaves

2 cups watermelon chunks

Directions

1. Place all of the ingredients into the Regular 24-ounce Cup in the order listed.
2. Select Auto-iQ™ Nutri Ninja® BLEND.
3. Remove blades from cup after blending.

NINJA KNOW-HOW

ADD 1/8 TEASPOON HOLY BASIL POWDER, ALSO CALLED TULSI, FOR A SUPER-FOOD BOOST.

PREP TIME: 5 minutes SERVINGS: 2 CONTAINER: Regular 24-ounce Cup

Kale K.O.

Ingredients

1/2 small ripe banana

1/4 cup cucumber chunks

3 tablespoons celery

1/4 cup parsley

Zest of 1 orange

1 cup kale

3/4 cup water

1/3 cup ice

1 cup frozen grapes

Directions

1. Place all of the ingredients into the Regular 24-ounce Cup in the order listed.
2. Select Auto-iQ™ Nutri Ninja® BLEND.
3. Remove blades from cup after blending.

NINJA® KNOW-HOW

ADD WALNUTS OR ALMONDS FOR A SUPER-FOOD BOOST.

PREP TIME: 5 minutes **SERVINGS:** 1 **CONTAINER:** Regular 24-ounce Cup

Butternut Squash Blast

Ingredients

3/4 cup butternut or acorn squash chunks, oven-roasted, cooled

3/4 cup unsweetened vanilla almond milk

1/8 cup shelled walnuts

1 1/2 teaspoons maple syrup

1 teaspoon ground turmeric

1/2 teaspoon cinnamon

1/2 cup ice

Directions

1. Place all of the ingredients into the Regular 24-ounce Cup in the order listed.
2. Select Auto-iQ™ Nutri Ninja® BLEND.
3. Remove blades from cup after blending.

DO NOT BLEND HOT INGREDIENTS.

PREP TIME: 5 minutes SERVINGS: 2 CONTAINER: Regular 24-ounce Cup

Ginger Pear Smoothie

Ingredients

1 ripe pear, cut in quarters, seeds removed

1 teaspoon fresh ginger

2 1/4 cups cold water

Sweetener, to taste

Directions

1. Place all of the ingredients into the Regular 24-ounce Cup in the order listed.
2. Select Auto-iQ™ Nutri Ninja® BLEND.
3. Remove blades from cup after blending.
4. Pour mixture through a fine-mesh strainer to extract the flavored water.
5. Store in refrigerator for up to 3 days.

PREP TIME: 5 minutes SERVINGS: 2 CONTAINER: Regular 24-ounce Cup

Ninja 9

Ingredients

1/2 cup English cucumber chunks

1/2 celery stalk, cut in quarters

1/4 Granny Smith apple, unpeeled, cut in chunks

1 small carrot, peeled, cut in quarters

1 tablespoon red onion

1/4 jalapeño, seeds removed

1/4 cup beet chunks

1/4 cup shredded red cabbage

1/4 teaspoon salt

1 cup tomato, cut in quarters

1/2 cup ice

Directions

1. Place all of the ingredients into the Regular 24-ounce Cup in the order listed.
2. Select Auto-iQ™ Nutri Ninja® ULTRA BLEND.
3. Remove blades from cup after blending.

NINJA KNOW-HOW

ADD 1 TABLESPOON MACA POWDER FOR A SUPER-FOOD BOOST.

PREP TIME: 5 minutes SERVINGS: 2 CONTAINER: Regular 24-ounce Cup

Frozen Kale Cacao

Ingredients

1 tablespoon unsweetened cocoa powder

3 dates, cut in half, pits removed

3/4 cup chopped kale leaves

1 cup unsweetened light coconut milk

1 small frozen ripe banana, cut in half

1/2 cup ice

Directions

1. Place all of the ingredients into the Regular 24-ounce Cup in the order listed.
2. Select Auto-iQ™ Nutri Ninja® ULTRA BLEND.
3. Remove blades from cup after blending.

NINJA KNOW-HOW

ADD 2 TABLESPOONS CACAO NIBS FOR A SUPER-FOOD BOOST.

PREP TIME: 5 minutes SERVINGS: 1 CONTAINER: Small 18-ounce Cup

You Make Me Bananas

Ingredients

½ orange, peeled, cut in half, seeds removed

¾ cup original flax milk

¼ teaspoon ground nutmeg

1 small frozen ripe banana, cut in half

Directions

1. Place all of the ingredients into the Small 18-ounce Cup in the order listed.
2. Select Auto-iQ™ Nutri Ninja® BLEND.
3. Remove blades from cup after blending.

PREP TIME: 5 minutes SERVINGS: 2 CONTAINER: Jumbo Multi-Serve 32-ounce Cup

Go Cocoa

Ingredients

1½ cups unsweetened coconut milk

4 tablespoons unsweetened cocoa powder

4 tablespoons whole almonds

4 dates, pits removed

2 small frozen ripe bananas, cut in half

1 cup ice

Directions

1. Place all of the ingredients into the Jumbo Multi-Serve 32-ounce Cup in the order listed.
2. Select Auto-iQ™ Nutri Ninja® ULTRA BLEND.
3. Remove blades from cup after blending.

PREP TIME: 5 minutes SERVINGS: 2 CONTAINER: Regular 24-ounce Cup

Carrot Tip-Top

Ingredients

1¼ cups carrot chunks

1 cup carrot juice

2 tablespoons ground flaxseed

½ cup silken tofu

1 cup ice

Directions

1. Place all of the ingredients into the Regular 24-ounce Cup in the order listed.
2. Select Auto-iQ™ Nutri Ninja® ULTRA BLEND.
3. Remove blades from cup after blending.

NINJA KNOW-HOW

ADD ½ TEASPOON RED CURRY PASTE FOR A SAVORY KICK.

PREP TIME: 5 minutes **SERVINGS:** 1 **CONTAINER:** Regular 24-ounce Cup

Ginger Greens

Ingredients

3/4 cup baby kale

1/4 cup fresh cilantro leaves

1/4 ripe avocado, peeled, pit removed

1 date, cut in half, pit removed

2 kiwis, peeled, cut in quarters

1 teaspoon lime juice

1/4-inch piece fresh ginger, peeled

1/4 cup coconut water

1/4 cup ice

Directions

1. Place all of the ingredients into the Regular 24-ounce Cup in the order listed.
2. Select Auto-iQ™ Nutri Ninja® ULTRA BLEND.
3. Remove blades from cup after blending.

PREP TIME: 5 minutes **SERVINGS:** 2 **CONTAINER:** Regular 24-ounce Cup

Apple Banana Green Smoothie

Ingredients

1 cup chopped Swiss chard, without fibrous stalk

1/2 cup parsley

1/4 cup sprouts of your choice

1 medium Golden Delicious apple, cored and cut up

2 teaspoons lemon juice

1/2 ripe banana

1/4 cup water

1/2 cup ice

Directions

1. Place all of the ingredients into the Regular 24-ounce Cup in the order listed.
2. Select Auto-iQ™ Nutri Ninja® ULTRA BLEND.
3. Remove blades from cup after blending.

NINJA KNOW-HOW

ADD 1 TEASPOON GELATINIZED MACA FOR A SUPER-FOOD BOOST.

PREP TIME: 5 minutes **SERVINGS:** 1 **CONTAINER:** Small 18-ounce Cup

Spinach Spectacular

Ingredients

1 1/2 cups spinach

1 tablespoon almonds

1/2 ripe avocado, pit removed

1/4 teaspoon cayenne pepper

1 1/4 cups unsweetened almond milk

2 scoops vanilla protein powder

1/2 cup frozen mango chunks

Directions

1. Place all of the ingredients into the Small 18-ounce Cup in the order listed.
2. Select Auto-iQ™ Nutri Ninja® ULTRA BLEND.
3. Remove blades from cup after blending.

NINJA KNOW-HOW

YOU CAN SUBSTITUTE ANY OF YOUR FAVORITE GREENS FOR THE SPINACH.

PREP TIME: 5 minutes **SERVINGS:** 1 **CONTAINER:** Regular 24-ounce Cup

Herbal Pear & Bok Choy Smoothie

Ingredients

3/4 cup chopped bok choy

1/4 cup fresh cilantro leaves

1 ripe pear, cored, cut in quarters

1/8 ripe avocado, peeled, pit removed

1 teaspoon lime juice

1/2 date, pit removed

1/4 cup brewed, chilled holy basil or tulsi tea

1/4 cup ice

Directions

1. Place all of the ingredients into the Regular 24-ounce Cup in the order listed.
2. Select Auto-iQ™ Nutri Ninja® ULTRA BLEND.
3. Remove blades from cup after blending.

DO NOT BLEND HOT INGREDIENTS.

NINJA KNOW-HOW

ADD 1/2 TEASPOON FLAXSEED OIL TO ROUND OUT THE FLAVORS.

PREP TIME: 5 minutes SERVINGS: 4–6 CONTAINER: 72-ounce Pitcher

Cran-Orange Splash

Ingredients

½ grapefruit, peeled, cut in quarters, seeds removed

1 orange, peeled, cut in quarters, seeds removed

2 kiwis, peeled, cut in half

½ cup fresh parsley leaves

2 cups cranberry juice

1¼ cups ice

Directions

1. Place all of the ingredients into the 72-ounce Pitcher in the order listed.
2. Select Auto-iQ™ FROZEN DRINKS/SMOOTHIES.

NINJA KNOW-HOW

CRANBERRIES FREEZE WELL SO YOU CAN STOCK UP ON THEM DURING THE HOLIDAYS AND USE THEM ALL YEAR LONG.

Infused Teas & Waters

Almond Chai Tea, page 46

PREP TIME: 5 minutes **SERVINGS:** 2 **CONTAINER:** Regular 24-ounce Cup

Almond Chai Tea

Ingredients

3 dates, cut in half, pits removed

2 tablespoons raw almonds

1/4 ripe banana

1 1/4 cups strongly brewed chai tea, chilled

Directions

1. Place all of the ingredients into the Regular 24-ounce Cup in the order listed.
2. Select Auto-iQ™ Nutri Ninja® ULTRA BLEND.
3. Remove blades from cup after blending.

DO NOT BLEND HOT INGREDIENTS.

PREP TIME: 5 minutes **SERVINGS:** 2 **CONTAINER:** Regular 24-ounce Cup

Tropical Fruit Tea

Ingredients

1/2 cup ripe papaya, cut in chunks

3 dried figs

1 1/2 cups cups strongly brewed mango passion fruit tea, chilled

1 cup frozen pineapple

Directions

1. Place all of the ingredients into the Regular 24-ounce Cup in the order listed.
2. Select Auto-iQ™ Nutri Ninja® BLEND.
3. Remove blades from cup after blending.

DO NOT BLEND HOT INGREDIENTS.

PREP TIME: 5 minutes **SERVINGS:** 2 **CONTAINER:** Regular 24-ounce Cup

Green Tea Tonic

Ingredients

1 cup red leaf lettuce

¼ cup cucumber chunks

2 (.035 ounce) packets stevia

1½ cups strongly brewed green tea, chilled

1 cup frozen mixed berries

Directions

1. Place all of the ingredients into the Regular 24-ounce Cup in the order listed.
2. Select Auto-iQ™ Nutri Ninja® ULTRA BLEND.
3. Remove blades from cup after blending.

DO NOT BLEND HOT INGREDIENTS.

NINJA KNOW-HOW ADD 1 TABLESPOON ALOE VERA JUICE FOR A SUPER-FOOD BOOST.

PREP TIME: 5 minutes **SERVINGS:** 1 **CONTAINER:** Small 18-ounce Cup

Cherry-Lime Rickey-ade

Ingredients

1 tablespoon lime juice

8 ounces coconut water

1/2 cup frozen cherries

Directions

1. Place all of the ingredients into the Small 18-ounce Cup in the order listed.
2. Select Auto-iQ™ Nutri Ninja® Blend.
3. Remove blades from cup after blending.
4. Pour mixture through a fine-mesh strainer to extract the flavored water. Serve over ice.

ADD 1 TABLESPOON CHIA SEED FOR YOUR OWN HOMEMADE CHIA FRESCA.

PREP TIME: 5 minutes **SERVINGS:** 2 **CONTAINER:** Regular 24-ounce Cup

Two Berry Tea

Ingredients

1 cup blueberries

2 tablespoons goji berries

½ ripe banana

1½ cups strongly brewed rooibos tea, chilled

1 cup ice

Directions

1. Place all of the ingredients into the Regular 24-ounce Cup in the order listed.
2. Select Auto-iQ™ Nutri Ninja® ULTRA BLEND.
3. Remove blades from cup after blending.

DO NOT BLEND HOT INGREDIENTS.

NINJA® KNOW-HOW

ADD 2 TABLESPOONS TART CHERRY CONCENTRATE FOR A SUPER-FOOD BOOST.

PREP TIME: 5 minutes **SERVINGS:** 2 **CONTAINER:** Regular 24-ounce Cup

Coconut Mango Energy-ade

Ingredients

3/4 cup mango chunks

1 teaspoon fresh mint leaves

2 cups coconut water

Directions

1. Place all of the ingredients into the Regular 24-ounce Cup in the order listed.
2. Select Auto-iQ™ Nutri Ninja® BLEND.
3. Remove blades from cup after blending.
4. Store in refrigerator for up to 3 days.

NINJA® KNOW-HOW

ADD 2 TABLESPOONS GROUND FLAXSEED FOR A SUPER-FOOD BOOST.

PREP TIME: 4 minutes **SERVINGS:** 2 **CONTAINER:** Regular 24-ounce Cup

Ginger Peach Lemonade

Ingredients

2 cups lemonade

1 1/3 cups frozen peach slices

1 teaspoon fresh ginger

Sweetener, to taste

Directions

1. Place all of the ingredients into the Regular 24-ounce Cup in the order listed.
2. Select Auto-iQ™ Nutri Ninja® BLEND.
3. Remove blades from cup after blending.

PREP TIME: 5 minutes **SERVINGS:** 2 **CONTAINER:** Regular 24-ounce Cup

Cherry Dragon Tea

Ingredients

1 1/2 cups strongly brewed cherry tea, chilled

1/4 teaspoon rose water

2 tablespoons honey

1 1/4 cups frozen dark sweet cherries

Directions

1. Place all of the ingredients into the Regular 24-ounce Cup in the order listed.
2. Select Auto-iQ™ Nutri Ninja® BLEND.
3. Remove blades from cup after blending.

DO NOT BLEND HOT INGREDIENTS.

NINJA KNOW-HOW ADD 2 TEASPOONS ACAI POWDER FOR A SUPER-FOOD BOOST.

Breakfasts

Trail Mix in a Glass, page 60

PREP TIME: 5 minutes **SERVINGS:** 1 **CONTAINER:** Small 18-ounce Cup

Top O' The Morning

Ingredients

½ orange, peeled, cut in quarters, seeds removed

½ small ripe banana, cut in quarters

½ cup unsweetened vanilla almond milk

¼ teaspoon ground cinnamon

1 scoop vanilla protein powder

¼ cup ice

Directions

1. Place all of the ingredients into the Small 18-ounce Cup in the order listed.
2. Select Auto-iQ™ Nutri Ninja® ULTRA BLEND.
3. Remove blades from cup after blending.

NINJA® KNOW-HOW

ADD 2 TEASPOONS GROUND FLAXSEED FOR A SUPER-FOOD BOOST.

PREP TIME: 10 minutes **COOK TIME:** 5 minutes **SERVINGS:** 2 **CONTAINER:** Jumbo Multi-Serve 32-ounce Cup

Tomato Basil Scramble

Ingredients

4 large eggs

1/4 cup vine-ripened tomato, seeds removed

1/4 cup mozzarella

1/4 cup fresh basil leaves

1/8 teaspoon salt

1/8 teaspoon ground black pepper

2 teaspoons unsalted butter

Directions

1. Place the eggs, tomato, mozzarella, basil, salt, and black pepper into the Jumbo Multi-Serve 32-ounce Cup. Hold down Auto-iQ™ PULSE until finely chopped.
2. Remove blades from cup after blending.
3. In a nonstick sauté pan, heat the butter over medium-high heat. Add the egg mixture, then cook, stirring frequently until fluffy and cooked through.

PREP TIME: 7 minutes **SERVINGS:** 2 **CONTAINER:** Regular 24-ounce Cup

Trail Mix in a Glass

Ingredients

1/4 cup raw unsalted almonds

1/4 cup raw unsalted pumpkin seeds

1 tablespoon raw sesame seeds

1/4 cup goji berries

1/4 cup pomegranate juice concentrate

1 1/4 cups unsweetened almond milk

3 tablespoons honey

1 cup ice

Directions

1. Place all of the ingredients into the Regular 24-ounce Cup in the order listed.
2. Select Auto-iQ™ Nutri Ninja® ULTRA BLEND.
3. Remove blades from cup after blending.

NINJA® KNOW-HOW

ADD 1 TABLESPOON SPANISH BEE POLLEN FOR A SUPER-FOOD BOOST.

PREP TIME: 5 minutes **SERVINGS:** 2 **CONTAINER:** Regular 24-ounce Cup

Strawberry Tofu Smoothie

Ingredients

2/3 cup silken tofu

2 tablespoons honey

1 1/4 cups unsweetened almond milk

1 cup frozen strawberries

Directions

1. Place all of the ingredients into the Regular 24-ounce Cup in the order listed.
2. Select Auto-iQ™ Nutri Ninja® BLEND.
3. Remove blades from cup after blending.

NINJA® KNOW-HOW

SUBSTITUTE ANY FROZEN FRUIT FOR ALMOST UNLIMITED TASTY VARIATIONS.

PREP TIME: 7 minutes **SERVINGS:** 2 **CONTAINER:** Regular 24-ounce Cup

Strawberry Sin-sation

Ingredients

1½ cups strawberries, cut in quarters, stems removed

1 tablespoon fresh mint leaves

1 teaspoon fresh ginger

1 tablespoon unsalted sunflower seeds

¾ cup pomegranate juice

½ cup coconut water

½ cup ice

Directions

1. Place all of the ingredients into the Regular 24-ounce Cup in the order listed.
2. Select Auto-iQ™ Nutri Ninja® BLEND.
3. Remove blades from cup after blending.

NINJA KNOW HOW

ADD 1 TABLESPOON TART CHERRY CONCENTRATE FOR A SUPER-FOOD BOOST.

PREP TIME: 6 minutes **SERVINGS:** 2 **CONTAINER:** Regular 24-ounce Cup

Orange Sunshine Splash

Ingredients

3/4 cup silken tofu

1/4 cup goji berries

1 orange, peeled, cut in half, seeds removed

1/4 cup orange juice

2 (.035 ounce) packets stevia

1 cup ice

Directions

1. Place all of the ingredients into the Regular 24-ounce Cup in the order listed.
2. Select Auto-iQ™ Nutri Ninja® BLEND.
3. Remove blades from cup after blending.

NINJA KNOW-HOW

ADD 1/4 CUP ALOE VERA JUICE FOR A SUPER-FOOD BOOST.

PREP TIME: 5 minutes **SET TIME:** 1 hour **COOK TIME:** 5 minutes **SERVINGS:** 4
CONTAINER: Jumbo Multi-Serve 32-ounce Cup

Buckwheat Boosted Pancakes

Ingredients

1 cup buttermilk

1 egg

3 tablespoons canola oil

½ cup buckwheat flour

½ cup all-purpose flour

1 teaspoon baking soda

1 teaspoon sugar

½ teaspoon salt

1 tablespoon honey

Directions

1. Place the buttermilk, egg and canola oil into the Jumbo Multi-Serve 32-ounce Cup.
2. Select Auto-iQ™ PUREE and blend for 5 seconds. Add the rest of the ingredients except for the honey, and blend for an additional 5 seconds. Add the honey, and blend for 5 more seconds.
3. Remove blades from cup after blending and let batter set for 1 hour.
4. On a lightly oiled griddle or sauté pan over medium heat, pour pancake batter in desired size and cook until small bubbles form. Flip and continue cooking until center is puffed and springs back when gently pushed.

PREP TIME: 5 minutes **SERVINGS:** 2 **CONTAINER:** Regular 24-ounce Cup

Coffee Soymoothie

Ingredients

1/2 cup strongly brewed decaf coffee, chilled

1/3 cup silken tofu

2 teaspoons almond butter

1/8 teaspoon cardamom powder

1 tablespoon agave nectar

1/2 cup ice

Directions

1. Place all of the ingredients into the Regular 24-ounce Cup in the order listed.
2. Select Auto-iQ™ Nutri Ninja® BLEND.
3. Remove blades from cup after blending.

DO NOT BLEND HOT INGREDIENTS.

NINJA® KNOW-HOW

ADD 1 TABLESPOON CACAO POWDER FOR A SUPER-FOOD BOOST.

Soups, Sauces & Entrées

Gazpacho, page 72

PREP TIME: 10 minutes **COOK TIME:** 35–40 minutes **SERVINGS:** 8 **CONTAINER:** 72-ounce Pitcher

Butternut Squash Soup

Ingredients

3 tablespoons olive oil

1 large yellow onion, chopped

1 cup raw cashews

1 large apple, peeled, cored, chopped

1 large carrot, peeled, chopped

2 pounds butternut squash, cubed

1 teaspoon fresh thyme leaves

1 bay leaf

4 cups vegetable stock, plus more to thin if desired

1/2 teaspoon salt, plus more to taste

Ground black pepper, to taste

Directions

1. Heat oil in a large saucepot and add the onions, cooking until they begin to soften, about 5 minutes. Add the cashews and cook, stirring, for about 5 minutes.
2. Add the chopped apple, carrot, squash, thyme, and bay leaf to the pot and cook for 5 minutes. Add the stock and stir to combine. Bring the soup to a boil and reduce the heat to medium-low, allowing to simmer until the squash is easily pierced with a knife, 20–25 minutes. Remove and discard bay leaf.
3. Allow soup to cool to room temperature. Working in batches, ladle the soup into the 72-ounce Pitcher. Turn unit ON and select Auto-iQ™ PUREE. Heat soup to desired temperature before serving.

DO NOT BLEND HOT INGREDIENTS.

PREP TIME: 15 minutes **COOK TIME:** 30 minutes **SERVINGS:** 4–6 **CONTAINER:** 72-ounce Pitcher

Curried Carrot Soup

Ingredients

2 teaspoons extra-virgin olive oil

3 cloves garlic, peeled, chopped

1 medium yellow onion, chopped

½ teaspoon salt

½ teaspoon ground black pepper

1 tablespoon red curry paste

2 cups chopped carrots

4½ cups low-sodium chicken broth

1 cup light coconut milk

Directions

1. In a stockpot at medium-low heat, add the oil, garlic, and onions. Cook for 5 minutes.
2. Add the salt, black pepper, red curry paste, carrots, and chicken broth. Bring to a boil, reduce the heat to medium-low, and cook for 20–25 minutes or until the carrots are fork-tender.
3. Remove from the heat, add the coconut milk, and cool to room temperature.
4. Place mixture into the 72-ounce Pitcher. Select Auto-iQ™ PUREE. Blend until smooth.
5. Return to pot and simmer until heated.

DO NOT BLEND HOT INGREDIENTS.

PREP TIME: 5 minutes, plus chilling time **SERVINGS:** 8 **CONTAINER:** 72-ounce Pitcher

Gazpacho

Ingredients

1 small red onion, cut in quarters

2 English cucumbers, chopped

1 yellow pepper, cut in quarters

1 red pepper, cut in quarters

3 pounds tomatoes, peeled, chopped, seeds removed

1 teaspoon minced garlic

4 tablespoons red wine vinegar

3 1/2 teaspoons salt

6 cups tomato juice

Directions

1. Working in batches, add the red onion, cucumber, peppers, and tomatoes to the 72-ounce Pitcher.
2. Hold down Auto-iQ™ PULSE until ingredients are finely chopped. Transfer to a large mixing bowl.
3. Add minced garlic, red wine vinegar, salt, and tomato juice and mix well.
4. Chill at least 3 hours before serving.

NINJA KNOW-HOW

CHILL COVERED IN THE REFRIGERATOR OVERNIGHT TO DEVELOP AND MELD FLAVORS.

PREP TIME: 5 minutes **SERVINGS:** 2 **CONTAINER:** Regular 24-ounce Cup

Salad on the Go

Ingredients

½ ripe pear, cut in half, seeds removed

1 tablespoon fresh mint leaves

1 cup baby arugula

1 cup original-flavor kombucha

1 cup ice

Directions

1. Place all of the ingredients into the Regular 24-ounce Cup in the order listed.
2. Select Auto-iQ™ Nutri Ninja® ULTRA BLEND.
3. Remove blades from cup after blending.

NINJA® KNOW-HOW

ADD 2 TEASPOONS SPIRULINA FOR A SUPER-FOOD BOOST.

PREP TIME: 10 minutes **COOK TIME:** 15 minutes **SERVINGS:** 2-4 **CONTAINER:** 72-ounce Pitcher

Red Pepper Soup

Ingredients

3 red bell peppers, roasted, peeled

1/4 cup sun-dried tomatoes

2 cloves garlic, peeled

1/4 cup white wine

1/4 bunch trimmed Italian parsley

1 cup low-sodium vegetable broth

Salt and pepper, to taste

Balsamic vinegar, as garnish

Directions

1. Place all of the ingredients into the 72-ounce Pitcher in the order listed.
2. Select Auto-iQ™ Puree.
3. Transfer to a medium saucepan and simmer until heated through, about 10 minutes. Serve hot in bowls garnished with a splash of balsamic vinegar, if desired.

DO NOT BLEND HOT INGREDIENTS.

PREP TIME: 15 minutes **COOK TIME:** 35 minutes **SERVINGS:** 6 **CONTAINER:** 72-ounce Pitcher

Kale & Celery Root Soup

Ingredients

2 teaspoons extra-virgin olive oil

2 cloves garlic, peeled, chopped

1 medium yellow onion, chopped

1 cup peeled, chopped celery root

2 cups chopped kale

1½ teaspoons salt

½ teaspoon ground black pepper

5 cups unsalted vegetable broth

Directions

1. In a 5-quart saucepot at medium-low heat, add the oil, garlic, and onions. Cook for 6 minutes.
2. Add the remaining ingredients, bring to a boil, reduce the heat to medium-low, and cook for 20–25 minutes or until the celery root is fork-tender.
3. Remove from the heat and cool to room temperature.
4. Place mixture into the 72-ounce Pitcher. Select Auto-iQ™ PUREE and blend until smooth.
5. Return to pot and simmer until heated.

DO NOT BLEND HOT INGREDIENTS.

NINJA® KNOW-HOW

ADD 1 TABLESPOON FLAXSEED FOR A SUPER FOOD BOOST.

PREP TIME: 5 minutes **SERVINGS:** 1 cup **CONTAINER:** Regular 24-ounce Cup

Pineapple Dipping Sauce

Ingredients

½ sweet white onion, cut in half

2 tablespoons fresh cilantro leaves

2 tablespoons lime juice

1 tablespoon coconut oil or other oil

½ small serrano chile, seeds removed

1 cup pineapple chunks

Salt and pepper, to taste

Directions

1. Place all of the ingredients into the Regular 24-ounce Cup in the order listed.
2. Select Auto-iQ™ PUREE and blend until smooth.
3. Remove blades from cup after blending.

NINJA® KNOW-HOW

WRAP CILANTRO IN A WET PAPER TOWEL AND STORE IN THE CRISPER DRAWER TO KEEP FRESH.

PREP TIME: 30 minutes **COOK TIME:** 30 minutes **SERVINGS:** 2–4 **CONTAINER:** 72-ounce Pitcher

Sun-Dried Tomato Sauce

Ingredients

1 onion, cut in quarters

4 cloves garlic, peeled

1 tablespoon canola oil

1 can (28 ounces) whole tomatoes and juice

6 ounces sun-dried tomatoes packed in olive oil

1/2 cup dry red wine

1/2 teaspoon red pepper flakes

1/4 bunch chopped basil (2 tablespoons reserved for garnish)

Salt and pepper, to taste

Directions

1. Place the onion and garlic into the 72-ounce Pitcher. Select Auto-iQ™ PULSE until roughly chopped.
2. Heat the oil in a medium saucepan over medium heat and sauté the onions and garlic for 5 minutes, until softened.
3. Add the tomatoes with juice, sun-dried tomatoes, red wine, and red pepper flakes to the 72-ounce Pitcher. Select LOW and blend for 15 seconds, until a chunky consistency is achieved.
4. Add the tomato sauce to the saucepan with the garlic and onions. Simmer for 20 minutes. Add fresh basil at the end.

DO NOT BLEND HOT INGREDIENTS.

NINJA® KNOW-HOW

YOU CAN SUBSTITUTE 8 RIPE ROMA TOMATOES FOR THE CANNED ONES—JUST SIMMER THEM FOR 2 HOURS.

PREP TIME: 10 minutes **SERVINGS:** 1¾ cups **CONTAINER:** Regular 24-ounce Cup

Passion Fruit Mustard Dressing

Ingredients

½ cup frozen passion fruit pulp, thawed

2 tablespoons Dijon mustard

¼ cup rice wine vinegar

3 tablespoons honey

2 tablespoons fresh thyme leaves

½ teaspoon salt

3 tablespoons extra-virgin olive oil

¾ cup fat-free sour cream

Directions

1. Place all of the ingredients into the Regular 24-ounce Cup in the order listed.
2. Select Auto-iQ™ PUREE and blend until smooth.
3. Remove blades from cup after blending.

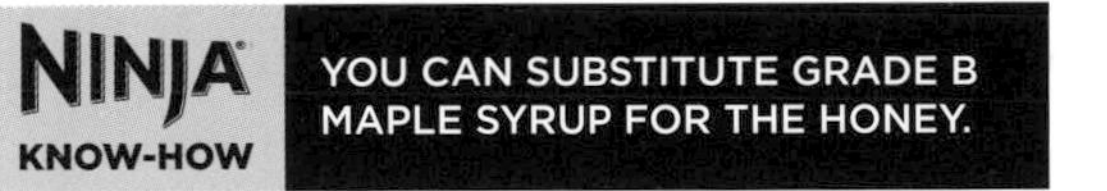

PREP TIME: 15 minutes **COOK TIME:** 15 minutes **SERVINGS:** 4 **CONTAINER:** Jumbo Multi-Serve 32-ounce Cup

Coconut Chicken in Orange Sauce

Ingredients

1 can (14 ounces) light coconut milk

2 cloves garlic, peeled

½ teaspoon salt

2 tablespoons green curry paste

4 6-ounce chicken breasts

½ cup orange marmalade

2 tablespoons prepared horseradish

Cornstarch, to coat

¼ cup vegetable oil

Directions

1. Place the coconut milk, garlic, salt, and curry paste into the Jumbo Multi-Serve 32-ounce Cup. Select Auto-iQ™ PUREE and blend until smooth.
2. Remove blades from cup after blending.
3. In an airtight container, place the chicken in the coconut mixture and marinate for 12 hours.
4. Preheat oven to 375°F.
5. In a mixing bowl, combine the marmalade and horseradish.
6. Remove chicken and drain excess marinade. Coat chicken in cornstarch.
7. In a nonstick sauté pan, heat the oil over medium-high heat. Add the chicken, then cook for 2 minutes per side. Remove chicken and place on a lined sheet pan that has been lightly coated with cooking spray. Bake for 10 minutes or until thoroughly cooked through.
8. Place chicken on a plate and serve with a side of the marmalade horseradish sauce.

PREP TIME: 10 minutes **COOK TIME:** 40–50 minutes **SERVINGS:** 2-4 **CONTAINER:** 72-ounce Pitcher

Butternut Mac & Cheese

Ingredients

1 pound butternut squash, peeled, cut in large pieces

1 cup water

1 cup low-fat milk

Salt and ground black pepper to taste

1 teaspoon dry mustard powder

3 cups cheddar cheese, shredded, divided

8 ounces elbow macaroni, cooked

1/4 cup bread crumbs

1/4 cup grated Parmesan cheese

2 teaspoons olive oil

Directions

1. Place the squash into the 72-ounce Pitcher. Select Auto-iQ™ PULSE until roughly chopped.
2. In a saucepan, place the squash, water, milk, salt, pepper, and mustard. Simmer for 20 minutes. Add 2 1/2 cups cheese and stir until melted. Cool to room temperature.
3. Add the cooled mixture to the 72-ounce Pitcher and select Auto-iQ™ PUREE.
4. Place cooked macaroni in a lightly buttered 2 1/2-quart baking dish. Pour squash mixture over macaroni. Toss bread crumbs, remaining cheddar cheese, Parmesan cheese, and oil and scatter over top.
5. Bake at 375°F for 20–25 minutes, until bubbly.

DO NOT BLEND HOT INGREDIENTS.

NINJA KNOW-HOW

USE LOW-FAT CHEDDAR CHEESE AND WHOLE WHEAT MACARONI AS FEEL-GOOD SWAPS.

PREP TIME: 4 minutes **SERVINGS:** 2 **CONTAINER:** Regular 24-ounce Cup

Waldorf Salad

Ingredients

1 cup chopped romaine lettuce

1/3 cup raw walnut halves

1 1/4 cups water

1 1/4 cups frozen red grapes

Directions

1. Place all of the ingredients into the Regular 24-ounce Cup in the order listed.
2. Select Auto-iQ™ Nutri Ninja® ULTRA BLEND.
3. Remove blades from cup after blending.

NINJA KNOW-HOW

ADD 4 ICE CUBES IF YOU DON'T HAVE FROZEN GRAPES ON HAND.

PREP TIME: 5 minutes **SERVINGS:** 6 **CONTAINER:** 72-ounce Pitcher

Blueberry Honey Cucumber Mojito

Ingredients

2 1/2 cups blueberries

1 cup chopped English cucumber

2 tablespoons fresh mint leaves

2 tablespoons honey

1 cup light rum

3/4 cup pear juice

3 cups ice

Directions

1. Place all of the ingredients into the 72-ounce Pitcher in the order listed.
2. Select Auto-iQ™ FROZEN DRINKS/SMOOTHIES.

NINJA® KNOW-HOW

ADD 1 TEASPOON FRESH GINGER FOR A SUPER-FOOD BOOST.

PREP TIME: 10 minutes **SERVINGS:** 4 **CONTAINER:** 72-ounce Pitcher

Strawberry Daiquiri

Ingredients

4 cups strawberries, hulled, cut in half

8 ounces lime juice

8 ounces light rum

2 cups ice

Directions

1. Place all of the ingredients in the 72-ounce Pitcher in the order listed.
2. Select Auto-iQ™ FROZEN DRINKS/SMOOTHIES.

PREP TIME: 10 minutes **SERVINGS:** 6 **CONTAINER:** 72-ounce Pitcher

Watermelon Basil Sangria

Ingredients

3 cups watermelon chunks

1/4 cup fresh basil leaves

2 limes, peeled, cut in half, seeds removed

1/2 cup brandy

1 cup dry white wine

3 tablespoons agave nectar

1 cup frozen peaches

2 1/4 cups ice

Directions

1. Place all of the ingredients into the 72-ounce Pitcher in the order listed.
2. Select Auto-iQ™ FROZEN DRINKS/SMOOTHIES.

NINJA® KNOW-HOW

MAKE THIS FRUITY DRINK WITH SPARKLING CIDER INSTEAD OF BRANDY AND WHITE WINE AS A GREAT FAMILY REFRESHER.

PREP TIME: 5 minutes **SERVINGS:** 4 **CONTAINER:** 72-ounce Pitcher

Lem-mosa

Ingredients

3 lemons, peeled, cut in half, seeds removed

2 tablespoons fresh mint leaves

1 3/4 cups sparkling wine

2 tablespoons agave nectar

3 1/2 cups ice

Directions

1. Place all of the ingredients into the 72-ounce Pitcher in the order listed.
2. Select Auto-iQ™ FROZEN DRINKS/SMOOTHIES.

NINJA® KNOW-HOW

ADD FRESH RASPBERRIES AS A GARNISH OR BLEND FOR A NEW TWIST.

PREP TIME: 10 minutes **SERVINGS:** 4 **CONTAINER:** 72-ounce Pitcher

Cool as a Cucumber

Ingredients

3 ounces London dry gin

1 cup chopped cucumber

4 mint leaves

2 ounces lime or lemon juice

2 ounces simple syrup or 1 ounce raw agave nectar

2 cups ice

Directions

1. Place all of the ingredients into the 72-ounce Pitcher in the order listed.
2. Select Auto-iQ™ FROZEN DRINKS/SMOOTHIES.

NINJA® KNOW-HOW

ADD 4 FRESH STRAWBERRIES FOR A TASTY AND COLORFUL VARIATION.

PREP TIME: 10 minutes **COOK TIME:** 20 minutes **SERVINGS:** 10–12 **CONTAINER:** 72-ounce Pitcher

Spinach & Artichoke Dip

Ingredients

1/4 cup mayonnaise

1/4 cup sour cream

8 ounces cream cheese

2 tablespoons lemon juice

1 can (14 ounces) artichoke hearts, drained and chopped

1/2 cup shredded low-fat mozzarella cheese

1/4 cup Parmesan cheese, grated or cut in pieces

2 tablespoons chopped onion

1 cup frozen spinach, thawed, excess liquid removed

Directions

1. Preheat oven to 350°F. Place all of the ingredients, except the spinach, into the 72-ounce Pitcher in the order listed. Select Auto-iQ™ PULSE until ingredients are combined.
2. Add the chopped spinach and continue to hold down Auto-iQ™ PULSE until incorporated. Spoon the dip into a heat-resistant serving dish and bake for 20 minutes. Serve with sliced French bread. Season with salt and pepper.

DO NOT BLEND HOT INGREDIENTS.

NINJA® KNOW-HOW

SUBSTITUTE LOW-FAT MAYONNAISE AND CREAM CHEESE FOR A LIGHTER OPTION.

PREP TIME: 5 minutes **SERVINGS:** 4 **CONTAINER:** 72-ounce Pitcher

Curry Bloody Mary

Ingredients

2 small celery stalks, cut in 1-inch chunks, plus extra stalk for garnish

1 lemon, peeled, seeds removed

4 small vine-ripened tomatoes, cut in quarters

1 cup carrot juice

2 teaspoons green curry paste

1 teaspoon tamarind concentrate

4 dashes hot sauce

Small pinch celery seed

4 ounces vodka

4 cups ice

Directions

1. Place all of the ingredients, except the ice, into the 72-ounce Pitcher in the order listed.
2. Select Auto-iQ™ FROZEN DRINKS/SMOOTHIES.
3. Serve over ice and garnish with celery stalk.

NINJA® KNOW-HOW

SERVE WITHOUT ALCOHOL FOR A DELICIOUS NUTRIENT EXTRACTION*.

*Extract a drink containing vitamins and nutrients from fruits and vegetables.

PREP TIME: 10 minutes, plus refrigeration **COOK TIME:** 25 minutes **SERVINGS:** 1¾ cups
CONTAINER: Small 18-ounce Cup

Farm Fresh Ketchup Relish

Ingredients

¾ cup yellow onion, cut in quarters, divided

½ red bell pepper, chopped, seeds removed

1 clove garlic, peeled

2 vine-ripened tomatoes, cut in quarters, seeds removed

1 tablespoon plus 2 teaspoons apple cider vinegar

½ teaspoon molasses

¼ teaspoon ground black pepper

¾ cup kosher baby dill pickles, cut in half

1 tablespoon Dijon mustard

Directions

1. Place ½ cup onion, red bell pepper, garlic, tomato, vinegar, molasses, and ground black pepper into the Small 18-ounce Cup. Select Auto-iQ™ PULSE and blend until smooth.
2. Remove blades from cup after blending.
3. Pour the tomato mixture into a 2-quart saucepot and cook at medium-low heat for 25 minutes, stirring occasionally.
4. Remove from the heat and pour into an airtight container and refrigerate for 1 hour.
5. Place the remaining ¼ cup onion, pickles, Dijon mustard, and the cooled tomato mixture into the Small 18-ounce Cup. Select Auto-iQ™ PULSE until desired chop.
6. Remove blades from cup after blending.

DO NOT BLEND HOT INGREDIENTS.

NINJA® KNOW-HOW

CHILL THE RELISH IN A COVERED CONTAINER OVERNIGHT TO HELP DEVELOP AND MELD THE FLAVORS.

PREP TIME: 15 minutes **SERVINGS:** 6 **CONTAINER:** Small 18-ounce Cup

Tabbouleh Dip

Ingredients

1/2 cup English cucumber, chopped

1/4 small yellow onion, cut in quarters

2 tablespoons fresh mint leaves

1/2 cup flat-leaf parsley leaves

1 1/2 vine-ripened tomatoes, chopped

1/4 teaspoon ground black pepper

1/4 teaspoon salt

1 tablespoon extra-virgin olive oil

1 tablespoon lemon juice

Directions

1. Place all of the ingredients into the Small 18-ounce Cup in the order listed.
2. Select Auto-iQ™ PULSE, and pulse until desired consistency is reached.
3. Remove blades from cup after blending.

SERVE THIS AS AN ACCOMPANIMENT TO GRILLED FISH, BEEF, OR LAMB.

PREP TIME: 25 minutes **SERVINGS:** 10 **CONTAINER:** Small 18-ounce Cup

French Onion Tofu Dip

Ingredients

1 tablespoon vegetable oil

1 medium yellow onion, chopped

½ teaspoon salt

¼ teaspoon ground black pepper

3 tablespoons malt vinegar

½ cup firm tofu

4 ounces fat-free cream cheese, softened

⅓ cup fat-free sour cream

Directions

1. In a 10-inch sauté pan at medium heat, add the oil, onion, salt, and black pepper. Cook for 6–8 minutes or until caramelized, stirring occasionally. Add the malt vinegar and cook for 1 minute.
2. Remove from the heat and let cool for 10 minutes.
3. Place the cooked onion mixture, tofu, cream cheese, and sour cream into the Small 18-ounce Cup.
4. Select Auto-iQ™ PULSE, and pulse until desired consistency is reached.
5. Remove blades from cup after blending.

DO NOT BLEND HOT INGREDIENTS.

Desserts

PREP TIME: 5 minutes, plus freezing **SERVINGS:** 4 **CONTAINER:** Regular 24-ounce Cup

Tropical Fresh Fruit Ice Pops

Ingredients

1 cup mango chunks

2 cups pineapple chunks

2 tablespoons agave nectar

Directions

1. Place all of the ingredients into the Regular 24-ounce Cup in the order listed.
2. Select Auto-iQ™ Nutri Ninja® BLEND.
3. Remove blades from cup after blending.
4. Pour into popsicle molds and freeze overnight or until solid.

NINJA KNOW-HOW

IF USING FROZEN MANGO, SELECT AUTO-IQ™ NUTRI NINJA® ULTRA BLEND.

PREP TIME: 5 minutes **SERVINGS:** 4 **CONTAINER:** Regular 24-ounce Cup

Choc-a-lot Frappe

Ingredients

1/3 cup silken tofu

1/2 cup 70% cacao dark chocolate

2/3 cup chocolate rice milk

1 (.035 ounce) packet stevia

2 cups ice

Directions

1. Place all of the ingredients into the Regular 24-ounce Cup in the order listed.
2. Select Auto-iQ™ Nutri Ninja® BLEND.
3. Remove blades from cup after blending.

NINJA KNOW-HOW

BLENDING TIME MAY VARY ACCORDING TO TEMPERATURE OF MILK.

PREP TIME: 5 minutes **SERVINGS:** 2 **CONTAINER:** Regular 24-ounce Cup

Banana Pudding

Ingredients

1 tablespoon white chia seeds

1/3 cup walnut halves

1/4 teaspoon ground cinnamon

1/4 teaspoon pure vanilla extract

1/2 cup original flavor rice milk

2 medium frozen ripe bananas, cut in half

Directions

1. Place the chia seeds in a container and add 1/3 cup water. Cover and place in the refrigerator overnight to soak.
2. Place all of the ingredients into the Regular 24-ounce Cup in the order listed.
3. Select Auto-iQ™ Nutri Ninja® BLEND.
4. Remove blades from cup after blending.

NINJA® KNOW-HOW

MAKE AHEAD AND KEEP COLD IN THE REFRIGERATOR UP TO 2 DAYS.

PREP TIME: 5 minutes **SERVINGS:** 4 **CONTAINER:** Regular 24-ounce Cup

Hawaiian Frappe

Ingredients

½ ripe banana

1 cup coconut water

1 tablespoon extra-virgin raw coconut oil

1 cup frozen pineapple chunks

1 cup ice

Directions

1. Place all of the ingredients into the Regular 24-ounce Cup in the order listed.
2. Select Auto-iQ™ Nutri Ninja® BLEND.
3. Remove blades from cup after blending.

NINJA KNOW-HOW

BLENDING TIME MAY VARY ACCORDING TO TEMPERATURE OF COCONUT WATER.

PREP TIME: 5 minutes **SERVINGS:** 1 **CONTAINER:** Small 18-ounce Cup

Lemon Strawberry Sorbet

Ingredients

3/4 cup lemonade

1 1/2 cups frozen strawberries

Directions

1. Place all of the ingredients into the Small 18-ounce Cup in the order listed.
2. Select Auto-iQ™ Nutri Ninja® ULTRA BLEND.
3. Remove blades from cup after blending.

PREP TIME: 5 minutes **SERVINGS:** 10–12 **CONTAINER:** Regular 24-ounce Cup

Monkey Business

Ingredients

1 ripe banana, cut in half

2 tablespoons unsweetened cocoa powder

1¼ cups original almond milk

1 tablespoon agave nectar

¼ cup almond butter

1 cup ice

Directions

1. Place all of the ingredients into the Regular 24-ounce Cup in the order listed.
2. Select Auto-iQ™ Nutri Ninja® BLEND.
3. Remove blades from cup after blending.

NINJA KNOW-HOW

ADD 2 TABLESPOONS CACAO NIBS FOR A RICH CHOCOLATE TASTE.

PREP TIME: 15 minutes, plus refrigeration **SERVINGS:** 4 **CONTAINER:** 72-ounce Pitcher

Banana Chocolate Mousse

Ingredients

2 ripe bananas, cut in quarters

2 ripe avocados, peeled, cut in quarters, pits removed

1/4 cup chocolate syrup

Juice of 1/2 orange

1/4 cup cocoa powder

Directions

1. Place all of the ingredients into the 72-ounce Pitcher. Select Auto-iQ™ PUREE and blend until smooth, scraping down Pitcher as needed.
2. Place mousse into an airtight container and refrigerate until chilled.

PREP TIME: 5 minutes **SERVINGS:** 2 **CONTAINER:** Jumbo Multi-Serve 32-ounce Cup

Vanilla Nut Frozen Treat

Ingredients

1/3 cup vanilla oat milk

1/4 cup walnut halves

1/4 teaspoon pure vanilla extract

1 packet (.035 ounce) stevia

1/3 cup nonfat vanilla yogurt

1 1/4 cups ice

Directions

1. Place all ingredients into the Jumbo Multi-Serve 32-ounce Cup in the order listed.
2. Select Auto-iQ™ Nutri Ninja® ULTRA BLEND.
2. Remove blades from cup after blending.

NOTES:

NOTES:

Index

Nutri Ninja® | Ninja® Blender Duo™
with Auto-iQ™ Technology

Simply Delicious, Simply Nutritious

75+ DELICIOUS RECIPES